MW00880302

About the Author

My name is Easton Allred. I am extremely fortunate to come from an incredible family with 4 sisters, my parents, and an epic brother in law. I am a huge believer in thinking outside the box. Furthermore, I am a top 10 nationally ranked runner for my age group. This year was one for the books, I had the opportunity to win the Colorado Junior Olympic race as well as the Nike Cross Southwest Regional Open race in Arizona. After about 5 years of passionate research on the topic of personal development, I discovered that through sharing my knowledge I could help others around me to have the same passion and motivation that I have. This is what lead me to start my podcast called Fueled For Teens. In this podcast I interview successful entrepreneurs, athletes, and philanthropists to determine what separates them from the greats. I've been honored to interview and learn from Caleb Maddix, Rich Roll, Jimmer Fredette, and many other people who have found greatness. The things that I have learned from these people and many other experiences in my life, are what have lead me to write this book.

Dedicated to my incredible family for loving and supporting me through this journey

INTRODUCTION

"Knowledge is not power, knowledge is only potential power. Action is power." - Tony Robbins

Something separates the average people from the greats, and I've spent the last few years of life learning it. I am obsessed with determining what makes Rich Roll, Steve Jobs, or Oprah different than the rest of us. This book, which I have put my heart and soul into, is the result of the vast studying that I have done through reading and listening to countless books, interviews, podcasts, keynotes. I have even done many interviews of my own, on my podcast, to find out all of the habits and tools that the most successful people in the world have used to get to where they are: the top.

This book is for the difference makers, the world changers, and the outside-the-box thinkers. Most of us are not there yet, but I believe that if you read and take to heart the contents of this book and believe in yourself, you can achieve anything. The first step towards great success is recognizing that you are capable of achieving it. When you start seeing yourself as difference maker, you start becoming one. When you set your mind on becoming a difference maker, your actions will automatically adjust to this new belief you have of yourself. You are special if you allow yourself to be. I am a firm believer that all of us have unique gifts and a purpose to apply those gifts. You are special and you were meant to achieve greatness. All you have to do is go and find it.

My purpose in writing this book is to help you become your greatest self and to help you achieve success. The tools and principles that lay in this book can be life changing if you choose to follow them. School teaches you a lot of great things, but it seems to leave out the most important piece: it doesn't teach you how to be successful in life. Rather, it teaches you the things necessary to fit into a job. School would rather have you learn the annual rainfall of Brazil than how to set and achieve goals and live the life of your dreams, or to find happiness. This book will teach you things of great importance, but they will not be effective unless you choose to allow them to be. Approach, therefore, is everything. I recommend that you approach this book with an open heart and a notebook in hand. Write down the things you learn and strive to make them part of your life. If you do this, your experience will be extraordinarily enhanced.

This book might be entertaining, but it's not meant for entertainment. It is meant to help you along the road to success—or get on it in the first place. Don't let this book become one of the many you buy every year and then put up on the shelf, yet another dust-gatherer in a life full of I'll-do-it-laters. If you want change, make it happen now. Tomorrow never comes.

MENTORS

"I look at where I am today and realize that most of my success is owed to the mentors that were in my life" - Kendrick Lamar

Inspired by Tai Lopez

Tai Lopez is a entrepreneur and motivational speaker that has made himself a fortune by utilizing the power of mentors. While speaking at a 2015 TED event Tai said, "Imagine that you had just started a business with Bill Gates as your business partner and he was using every trick of the trade that he used to build to Microsoft into one of the biggest companies in the world. How much money would you have today if Warren Buffet was teaching you how to invest in the stock market, showing you what he used to build Berkshire Hathaway into a 140-billion-dollar company. Imagine how much happier you would be today if the Dalai Lama was your personal guide showing you how to find happiness in the little things in life that most people overlook. Imagine how much healthier you would be today, if you woke up, went down to the gym, and Arnold Schwarzenegger was waiting there as your personal trainer, showing you how he built his body to maybe the fittest ever. Imagine the change you would be making in the world, the injustice you'd be solving today if Mother Teresa and you were running a charity together and she was showing you what she learned on the streets of Calcutta, helping the poor, the sick, and the dying." - Tai Lopez.

This excerpt is the very beginning of Tai Lopez's legendary TED talk about mentors. Today, he has millions of followers across social media, lives in Beverly Hills, and owns more than one Lamborghini—but it didn't all start out like that. When Tai was 16 years old, he began looking at who he wanted to become. He needed some direction and answers. He realized that life was too complex to figure out on his own, so he decided to write a letter seeking the answers to all of life's questions to the smartest person he knew: his grandpa. To Tai's disappointment, his grandpa refused to give him the answers: "Tai, the modern world is too complicated. You'll never find all the answers from just one person. If you're lucky, you'll find a handful of people throughout your life who will point the way."

A week later Tai found a package on his door with a note that read: "Start with these." Inside the package, he found eleven long books. Little did he know that these books would begin a chain reaction that would change his life. These books got him fired up to search wholeheartedly for what he calls "the good life."

The next few years for Tai were mainly a series of experiments. He read hundreds of books. He went to live with the Amish. The Amish are traditionalist Christians who purposefully live without electricity, cars, or any of the modern technology that we enjoy today. After two years with the Amish, Tai joined the long list of entrepreneur college dropouts and completely ran out of money. As a result, he had to sleep on the couch of his mom's mobile home. People with no college degree, no marketable skill, and no money who sleep on the couch of their mom's mobile home wish they were as high as rock bottom. But Tai had not given up yet. He remembered his grandpa's advice to find a few people that he could learn from. He grabbed the yellow pages, scrolled until he found the biggest ad in the book and decided that he was going to meet this person.

He borrowed a suit, got a friend to drive him and went to go meet this man—a man who he knew nothing about. When he arrived he walked straight into the man's office and proposed that he would work for this man for free if the man would teach him how to be successful. He gave himself up for knowledge. He was willing to do whatever it took to find the good life. To his surprise, the man said, "Tai, I have been looking for someone like you for 20 years." Tai's life would never be the same. He learned all he could from the man in the yellow pages and went on to learn from many other seven-figure-earning entrepreneurs. A few years later, Tai became one of the most successful entrepreneurs on the planet. To outsiders, it would've looked like a lucky accident, but he had put in the hard work for years to put himself in that position. The Ferraris, Lamborghinis, and mansions that he had always dreamed about became a reality. Today, Tai is well-known for reading a book a day everyday. He dedicates his life to teaching others how to find and properly utilize mentors.

Your ability to find and use mentors is the biggest predictor of your future success. If you can do this, you will have so many doors opened for you. I have personally experimented a great deal with who your time should be spent with. The best way to balance your time is with the "law of 33 percent." One third of your time should be spent with those who are (in a sense) below you, or behind you. These are people that you can mentor. The second third of your time should be spent with people that are similar to you both in success and the stage of their life they find themselves in. The final third of your time should be spent with those who can mentor and guide you on the road to success. Jim Rohn said it best: "You are the average of the five people you spend the most time with." It is critical, especially in our formative teenage years in the midst of high school, that we are spending time with the people that will bring us up rather than drag us down. One third, one third and one third: don't forget it.

WHY?

What can we learn from Tai's story? First, mentors bring success. It's easy for us to see that it would be impossible to be an NBA player without ever having a coach. No gymnast could become an Olympian and master their perfect technique without someone showing them how. Hollywood directors spend years learning under established directors before they direct their first film. Why don't we take greater advantage of these mentors? Most of us are blessed to have coaches, teachers, and parents that can guide us on our journey. A huge part of this book is about finding your purpose and going after it. If your purpose is to be a coach or teacher, then find the best coach or teacher you know and learn everything you can from them. If, like me, you don't, you need to find somebody that is where you want to be in five-ten years and ask for their help.

Right now I have a mentor that I meet with every other Wednesday. We usually spend about 30 minutes talking about my accomplishments over the last two weeks and things that I can do in the following weeks to multiply my business. As an entrepreneur, there are countless unknowns. Sometimes I wish that starting your own business were like math homework: there's only one answer, you follow a series of definite steps and you find that answer, and then you've successfully completed your math homework. The difficult thing about entrepreneurship, as with many things in life, is that there are no set steps that will guarantee success. There is no direct formula to a successful business. It's risky. But sometimes it's the risky things in life that reap the greatest rewards. Anybody can do math, but not anybody is willing to take the risk of not just entrepreneurship, but anything that is abnormal, anything that would set you apart from everyone else. No successful person ever got where they are now because of normal. But don't let me mislead you: you don't automatically become successful by doing things that are undiscovered and risky. You have to figure out what's going to work and what isn't. This is why having a business coach or mentor has been so life changing for me. They can see things that you cannot see. They can act as connectors. They can give you information that can be found nowhere else. They can be a fantastic source of motivation and encouragement. Mentors know the path. They've been further down the path, and they've come back to get you and guide you along it.

This idea that mentorship can change your future is what motivated me to start my podcast, Fueled For Teens. My passion is heavily focused around athletics and entrepreneurship. On my podcast, I get to interview people who have reached my all-time goals already. These people know the way that I am so eager to find. You will never find your treasure without the map. Sometimes the best way to get that map is to borrow it from someone else. Every successful person has mentors. Tony Robbins, who is already a billionaire, has several mentors and meets with them every day. Albert Einstein met with his mentor every Thursday. Oprah Winfrey, Gandhi, Benjamin Franklin, Jay-Z—even Spiderman!—all have mentors. Alexander the Great had Aristotle. Bill Gates had Paul Allen. Warren Buffet had Benjamin Graham. No matter who you are or what you are doing, mentors can have a life-changing influence on you.

HOW?

So we've established that everyone needs a mentor to be successful, and you are no exception. But how do you find—and keep—a mentor? Three or so years ago, I attended an entrepreneurship event in San Diego called "Life on Fire". While I was the youngest person at the event by a decent margin, I still spent the two days connecting with and learning from as many people as I could. This all happened before I had started my business or my podcast. I hadn't really done much at this point, but I was ambitious. While I didn't have much to show for, I was passionate and eager to learn. I believe this is why Kevin Stimpson, a highly successful entrepreneur and branding expert, offered to mentor me. I met Kevin on the first day of "Life on Fire" and knew he was going to be a part of my life for a long time. This guy has the most incredible energy and passion for what he's doing. He has also had some major success doing the things that I wanted to do—that is, start a business.

On the last day of the event, Kevin told me that he wanted to mentor me. I said yes, and thank goodness I did. You see, It doesn't take being prodigy, it takes ambition and tenacity. I wasn't incredibly successful, but I had the aspiration and dedication. I had demonstrated that dedication by flying alone to entrepreneurship event where everyone was over ten years older than me. Kevin wanted to give back. Successful people often want to give back. I didn't even have to ask him to be my mentor! His mentorship has played a huge role in where I am today and will continue to do so.

So how do you find a mentor that will help guide you to success? My first piece of advice is to find something that you absolutely love, pursue it relentlessly, and then let your desired mentor see just how passionate you are about it and just how authentic—authenticity is important—your passion and drive really are. Find someone who is good at something you want help with.

Secondly, in your search for a mentor, you have to keep in mind that while there certainly are people like Kevin who want to give back, not everyone is going to be as generous as he was. Most, in fact, will not. Whether we like it or not, most people are looking to benefit themselves. The most efficient way to find a mentor is to look at how you can add value to them. If Tai Lopez had walked into the man in the Yellow Pages office and asked to be mentored without offering work in return, it's very likely the man would have kicked him out of his office, and Tai would still be living on his mom's couch. But Tai offered to work for this man for free. He brought value to the mentorship. Few people will be willing to help you if you do not bring some kind of value to the relationship. This, in fact, is a key concept in any area of your life. Adding value is the key to any successful relationship, whether it's a mentorship, friendship, or relationship. Always be thinking of how can you add to the other person. The successful mentors we want value their time more than anything. Most successful people would rather give you a check than allow you to take their time to mentor you. This is part of the reason why building a relationship is so important. I have a buddy, Casey Adams, who is 17 years old and has built a following of almost 100k across social media. He has also been mentored by some of the biggest names in entrepreneurship. When I asked him what his secret to his success was, he said he owed it all to his ability to connect with powerful influences. The most effective way he found to do this was build a relationship little by little with the people that he desired to meet. He would comment on every Instagram picture of Tai Lopez and DM him weekly thanking him for his inspiration. He never asked for anything and then one day, Tai responded and invited Casey to come to Beverly Hills and film with him. If you want to have great mentors, you have to be persistent in building a relationship little by little.

If I told you that I was having a dinner at my place and Mahatma Gandhi, Nelson Mandela, Oprah Winfrey, Muhammad Ali, and Michael Phelps were all going to be there answering questions and spilling all the secrets that they used to change the world, would you be there? Obviously, the answer would be yes. Imagine how much value would be in that room. Your life would change forever. Everyone would want to come. In fact, my house would be overflowing with people. The thing is all of these people can be at my house. Not in person, but through books. The average American buys 17 books every year, but only reads about 3. What an unfortunate waste of knowledge. Tai Lopez reads a book a day and has practically made a living off of the things he has learned from books. Sam Walton made 160 billion dollars. He was the richest man in America. In the last year of his life he wrote a book that retails for $5. A lifetime of knowledge from a self-made multi-billionaire is sitting there unread on a bookshelf, gathering dust like all the other books. While we don't necessarily need to read a book a day, a book every two weeks should be a goal for us all. Imagine how much more knowledge you would gain if you went from reading three books a year to twenty-six.

When searching for a mentor, don't be afraid to go big. If you want to make a million dollars, find someone who makes ten million dollars. Apply the ten-times rule. Find someone that is ten times better than where you want to be and follow their lead. You'd be surprised at the diverse range of people you could use as a mentor. Many of the world's top entrepreneurs, business men, and athletes have had huge mentors from a young age. I have seen this in my own life. Some of the people I have had on my podcast would seem to most people, unattainable, but I made it happen. This is why I was able to have Rich Roll (named one of the top 25 most fit men on Earth), Caleb Maddix (Top 30 Under 30 entrepreneur),

Jimmer Fredette (BYU basketball star), and John Lee Dumas (multi-millionaire entrepreneur), on my podcast.

Caleb Maddix is a 15 year old entrepreneur that is creating tidal waves in the personal development industry. When I first started my podcast, I direct messaged him on Instagram multiple times. I direct messaged his dad. I commented on all of his posts. I even managed to find his email address and attempted to contact him there. None of this worked. Then, an opportunity arose. Caleb announced that he was giving a TED talk in Greeley Colorado, which was about three hours from my where I live. I immediately purchased VIP tickets and talked my mom into driving me down there. The next day, as Caleb was prepping for his TED talk, I found the speakers room and asked Caleb to be on my podcast. He was more than willing. I was determined and in the end I was successful.

A famous real estate investor has a similar story. Let's call him Joe. When Joe was 19 he decided that he wanted to work in real estate, so he did some research and found the office of the best developer in town. Joe went up to his secretary and asked to schedule a meeting. To his disappointment, she told him that he was a busy man and had no time to meet with him. For the next 17 days in a row he went back asking to meet his man, and every time he got the exact same response. Finally, on the 18th day, Joe went to the secretary as usual—but that day he got a different response. She felt bad for him, so she said, "Listen, here is what you do. Hide behind the plant by the elevator, when he comes out of the office at the end of day, jump in the elevator with him and he won't have a choice, the doors will close. Then, you will have four floors to convince him that you're worth talking to." While we don't know exactly what Joe said, we know he said enough to make the developer to say, "Meet me at the airport in the morning, we will take a private jet down to Florida, and I'll show you how I invested in hotels down there." This series of events lead Joe to be mentored by one of the greatest real estate investors in the US. Persevere, try, fail, try again—and fail and try again and fail and try again. Perseverance will set you apart from all the other people trying to get something from the people at the top.

BE A MENTOR

Remember how we talked about the 33 percent rule? We still have yet to talk about why it is so important to be a mentor to others. Over the past few years, I have had good and bad mentors, but the ones that have probably had the most influence on me are the ones that I have now in high school. Whether you know it or not, there is always someone watching you. As a freshman, I spent a lot of time this year figuring out how things work. I watched every move of the kids who I thought were worth learning from. Some of the kids on the varsity basketball and track teams have had a much larger impact on me than they would imagine. Has someone you really looked up to told you that they believed in you?

I have been blessed to have a couple of these people in my life and it has changed my world to have someone that I look up to believe in me. It would make my day even when they said "Hi" to me —but, conversely, when some of them weren't so friendly it hurt a lot more. Never forget that you are having that impact on somebody else who looks up to you. You can change people's lives if you under-stand this responsibility that everybody has at some point in their life. Choose your actions carefully and never underestimate the damage that being unkind to someone who looks up to you can do—or the po-tential good a simple greeting, a compliment or a word of encouragement can do. Your efforts as a mentor also helps you to learn. It forces you to think about what worked for you. When you teach, you be-gin to learn things better than ever before.

GOAL SETTING

People with clear, written goals, accomplish far more in a shorter period of time than people without them could ever imagine.

Inspired by: "12 weeks in a Year" and Brian Tracy

When I was 10 years old, I had a major life transition. I discovered one of my grandest passions. This was the passion for personal development and goal setting. One day, my mom was listening to a podcast episode by Brian Tracy a guy I had never heard of before. In this episode, Brian was talking about goal setting and how to set your goals properly to achieve them in the shortest amount of time. This podcast episode is what shaped the person that I am today. My mom introduced these goal-setting ideas to me, and I began to implement them immediately. From that day on I wrote my goals down every single day and it changed my life. I would not be anywhere near the person I am today without this experience. These goals started that chain reaction that led me to my desire to become an expert in personal development. My hope is that through reading this chapter, you will be able to transform your life and achieve your wildest goals and aspirations. I not only hope that this is possible, but I believe it.

How many of you have set New Year's resolutions? My guess is that all of you have at some point in your life. Every year, the entire world stops to set goals for the New Year, but how many people actually keep these goals? Statistics show that by the 15th of January in the new year 95 percent of people have already dropped their goals. That is, if they have even made it to setting goals in the first place. In fact, many of you have been stuck in this statistic. Year after year, you set goals and year after year it fails, so why even bother? If we know we are going to fail, why do we keep on trying? The human desire to be great and to improve is incredibly strong. The only way to find happiness in your life is through progress. Progress is happiness. Much of the time there is way too much emphasis on change. With the new year everyone is seeking change rather than progress. Change comes no matter what you do—it's automatic. The weather changes, your age changes, the economy changes. When many of us set our goals we say, "I am working on change." Or, "I want to change." The focus should instead be on making progress towards improving ourselves.

For most people, resolutions or goals become wish lists. It becomes a list of things that we just hope will magically happen. To set a resolution is to resolve to do something. When you resolve to do something you are focused on nothing else but that goal. If you really want to become successful and transform your life, the first thing you need to do is make your goals a need rather than a want. Everyone in life achieves their needs! Everyone! But your wants are illusory. This is a mistake that I made with my goals for a very long time. If you want to take the island, burn the boats. Take away any chance to go back, and then you will have no choice but to make sure that you achieve your goal.

Do any of you have asthma? Have you ever had an asthma attack? If you have, you know what it's like to want something bad. When you are having an asthma attack, all you want is to breathe! You don't care about what's going on in the news or how many likes you got on your instagram post. All you care about is breathing and you will do absolutely anything for just one breath. When you want to succeed as bad as you want to breathe in that moment, then you will be successful. There's a single question that has kept me fueled for so many years: How bad do you want it? I ask myself this question everyday. In fact, I have a poster on my door as a reminder. In my middle school cross country state meet a few years ago, someone from the side of the course yelled it out at me: How bad do you want it?! I decided that I wanted it more than anybody else. I pushed past every mental barrier to do what had to be done. The person who wants it more is always going to get it. So: how bad do you want it?

Recently, I have spent a large amount of time contemplating standards. You will always be consistent with the person that you believe you are. Everyone sets standards for themselves and most of the time it is subconscious. Much like how everyone achieves their needs, everyone will stay consistent with their standards. When Michael Jordan was asked for the secret to his historic career he gave a simple answer. I don't know what this reporter was expecting, maybe steroids, super power juice or something. Instead, Michael Jordan said that he held himself to a standard that nobody else would find humanly possible. Michael Jordan expected nothing less than to be the best and he always held himself to that standard. For some, this becomes a major advantage in life, but for most, it is probably the most crippling fact of our time. Self doubt plagues us or confidence fuels us. Which do you choose?

When elephants are being raised for the circus, they are tied up to a stake in the ground that is impossible to move. These little elephants spend much of their first few days fighting tooth and nail with that stake, doing whatever they can to rip it out of the ground—but they never pull it out. After a day or two, the elephant gives in. Years later, when they're ready for the circus, they are tied to that same stake, but now they are 2,000 pounds of muscle. They could rip that stake out with extraordinary ease. But here's the crazy thing: the elephant never tries. It stays prisoner to something it could destroy in a second. Why is this? Because of previous experience, this elephant doesn't believe it can pull out this stake. It has set an expectation for itself, and it doesn't exceed that expectation. As humans, we do this to ourselves as well. You will come to know that mind is powerful beyond your imagination. We will achieve what we believe. Self doubt destroys lives, careers, and our happiness.

One of my greatest "pet peeves" is when somebody says that they are just not that type of person, or that they can't do something. Whenever you have the urge to say, "I can't" or "I'm not" ask yourself this: When did I define myself? When did you decide what you could and couldn't do? When did you decide that you were dumb, slow, or just unable to do things right? Stop telling yourself these things right now. Beliefs are powerful. Here is how you change your beliefs: practice positive self talk. Your brain has between 40 and 60 thousand thoughts per day. All day long, you are talking to yourself. You are telling yourself a story, and you will be a direct result of whatever that story is. It may be difficult at first, but make sure to demolish any negative self talk in your head. Change I can't to I am. This may sound ridiculous, but I always follow after Lightning McQueen before my races. Before and even during my races I constantly talk to myself: "I am speed, I am the best runner in this race, I can endure the most pain." Many people have told me that I am only good at running because of a natural talent. What do I have to say to that? That's straight up bull crap. Yes, I have natural talent. But this sport is as much mental as it is physical, and I do the simple— and, yes, weird—things that nobody else is willing to do. That's why I'm successful. Anybody can run. But not everybody can cheer themselves to run on and it makes all the difference.

How to Find Your Passion

Our passions are what make our lives so great. It becomes near impossible to be happy if you are not living out your passions. In this section, my goal is to set you up so that you can discover your passions, and then later we will set goals based off of those passions. When I was in sixth grade, during math class, my teacher went off topic and started talking about nutrition and what foods we need to eat to keep us healthy. At the time, all I knew about nutrition was that sugar was bad, but as my teacher was talking about it, I got giddy. I wanted to jump out of my chair because I was so excited. Some of you reading this are thinking: What the heck? This kid is weird. And you are right: I am a little weird. But I guarantee this has happened to you at some point in your life. After that giddy excitement I felt about nutrition, I knew that wherever I was going in the future, I wanted nutrition and health to be apart of it. I knew that I wanted to learn everything I could on the topic.

A few years earlier, during the third grade, I had a similar experience with gardening and personal development. I had gone over to my friend's house after a day of school and at his house I found the coolest garden I had ever seen. This tower garden was an indoor, vertical, dirt-less garden that watered itself. I became obsessed. I absolutely loved this new thing. That same day I talked my mom into getting one for our family. Seeing how obsessed with this tower garden I was, my friends asked me if I would be interested in selling them and making $100 from every sale. One hundred dollars seemed like crazy money, so I eagerly accepted. This single experience felt insignificant at the time, but it proved later on the be extraordinarily impactful in my life. The funny thing is, I am not really a salesperson or a professional gardener. I am passionate about sales and gardening, but the most important part was that this experience

25

opened the door for me to personal development. When my grandma found out I was attempting to sell tower gardens, she sent me a boatload of personal development talks and books. I ate it all up. Reading all of these things I could do to make my life ten times better got me so fired up. This is what lead me to attending business conferences, watching TED events, reading countless books, and learning just about everything there was to learn about personal development and creating your best self.

We are all born with passions. It's part of our nature. I found that the most effective way to find your passions are to look for them. In one word, explore. Search for the things that make your heart sing. That is step one. Step two is to write down those things that make your heart sing so that you do not forget them. Step three is to decide which passions excite you enough to become an expert in them— and then to go after them.

Why So Important?

The Harvard MBA program is one of the most difficult programs in the country to get into. The acceptance rate today is about 15 percent. These students are traditionally successful and standout people. In 1979, interviewers asked new graduates from the Harvard MBA program this question: "Have you set clear, written goals for your future and made plans to accomplish them?" The results made history and became one of the most talked about studies in personal development. These interviewers found that 84 percent of these students had no specific goals. Another 13 percent had goals, but had not committed them to paper. The final three percent of students had clear, written-down goals. The 13 percent of the class who had goals were earning, on average, twice as much as the 84 percent who had no goals at all. Even more staggering—the three percent who had clear, written goals were earning, on average, ten times as much as the other 97 percent put together. Did you get that? The 3 percent made ten times more money than the other 97 percent of already successful students combined. The people around you may be smarter, faster, stronger, and better-looking than you are, but if you write down your goals, you will win that battle every time. This study ultimately shows how important goal setting is and how transformational it can be—even at the top.

Without a map you will never find treasure and without goals you will never find greatness. A few months ago, my mom said something I will never forget: "The world moves out of the way for those who know what they want." If you are not going after your dreams, then you will be going after somebody else's. If you do not define what you want, somebody will for you. There is no possible way to find success if you have no clue what success for you is. When I first started setting goals, I started achieving them and I started to find a purpose. Even if you don't know every single detail of what you want in life, the most important thing is to get started. Start, and it will be much easier for everything else to fall into place.

How?

Here we go! If you only read one little section of this book, it should be this one right here. We already know how important it is to to set goals, so let's make it happen. Many of you may be wondering why someone like me—a 15-year-old boy—should teach you how to set your goals. First of all, I would not tell who how to set goals if I were simply guessing. I have been a participant in many different goal-setting courses from people like Chalene Johnson, Lewis Howes, Darren Hardy, Brian Tracy, and Michael Hyatt, all of whom make millions every year. Unfortunately, as a teen, I have found that each of these tactics and ways to set goals were either much too complicated or missing pieces. I have taken everything I learned from these individuals and created my own personal goal-setting method that is specifically designed for teens. Second of all, I have seen this method of setting goals pay off way more than even I could have ever imagined. By writing down my goals every single day, I have been able to accomplish the seemingly impossible—and so will you.

Goal setting can be extremely tedious, but I want to challenge you all to enjoy this. Dream big and love the process. Most importantly of all, get it done. Set aside an hour or two to just completely knock this out. There have been so many times where I have come up with excuses to put this off and it has wrecked me. I find that the happiest times in my life are when I have clear, specific goals. No matter what month, what stage of life, or what circumstances you are in, you need to set goals today or else tomorrow will become a year from now. Please, I am begging you for your own sake: get this done now. Once you are done, DM me on instagram saying that you have finished setting your goals at @eastoncreedallred. Finally, set goals that pull you. Set goals that make you want to jump out of bed with eager passion to achieve them. Your goals should be a little insane. They should be possible, but a stretch. If your goals do not excite you, it is going to be extremely difficult to achieve them. Dream big, work hard, achieve the impossible.

SMART GOALS

S.pecific | Your goals should not be broad.

M.easurable | Every goal you set must be measurable.

A.greed upon | Find someone to keep you accountable.

R.ealistic | Dream big, but within reach. Then, dream bigger.

T.imely | Have a specific date that your goal must be completed.

Step One: Write out all of your long term goals and dreams. Your main goal is to develop a vision for yourself. No goal is too big—just imagine and dream your ideal life. What do you want your life to look like in 10 to 20 years? What do you want to have accomplished? You are just brainstorming ideas for now, not concerned at all with how you are going to get there. You should be able come up with at least 15 different things you would want in your dream future.

Step 2: Rank eight areas of your life according to how well you feel you are doing. These areas are displayed below. All you are going to do is put a number from one to ten, depending on how well you feel you are doing in that area. The areas you rank the lowest in are likely the things that are most important to you and may also need the most work. You will set your goals based off of these rankings.

Step Three: This step where it all starts to happen, so make it count. This step will create your future. You are going to write down your 4 goals that you want to achieve in a year. These 4 goals should follow the acronym S.M.A.R.T and they should be moving you towards your dream life that you created for yourself.

Step Four: In step 4, you are going to do divide your 4 goals into 4 different sections of the year. Each goal get's its very own 12 weeks. In these 12 weeks you are going to fight tooth and nail to achieve your goal. I have spend way too much time in my life fighting for 20 goals and I have often ended up achieving none. Fully immerse your focus on one thing and you will undoubtedly achieve it. Entrepreneurs like Tony Robbins, and John Lee Dumas have dedicated their lives to goal setting and have come to the same conclusion (1 goal at a time works best). Based on the research I have done on the topic of goal setting, the most effective strategies follow those who have only 1 goal at a time. At first this idea seemed crazy to me, after all, I then had 10 different goals and was spinning a million different plates. Fully immerse yourselves every twelve week period and your life will be transformed.

Step Five: The final step is to develop a plan to achieve these goals. There are a variety of ways to do this. Here are some suggestions: Write down step by step roadmaps for your goal, and have a checklist for what you want to get done each day that will take you towards that goal.

Complete all of these steps today and begin the journey to the new you. The trick to staying honest in all of your goals is to keep an accountability partner. I have seen so many times where accountability in goal setting has made all the difference. A few years ago, I decided that I wanted to do my own workout circuit everyday. This was about the tenth time I had set this goal, and I had failed every other time. But this time I decided to get an accountability partner, and this time I succeeded in my goal. One of my best friends was on my basketball team and we both wanted to be bigger and stronger to keep up with the competition, so he joined in the challenge. We texted each other every night to confirm that we had achieved our simple goal for the day. The most effective way to use an accountability partner is to share your plan of action rather than to share the actual end goal. Studies have shown that accountability partners increase your likelihood of achieving a goal by 85 percent.

In addition, sometimes sharing the actual goal, rather than the plan, can be ineffective. Many goal setting strategists believe and have proven that when you share your goal with someone, it gives you a false sense of achievement and strips some of your motivation. However, I do know many people who share both their goal and their plan with and accountability partners and it has turned out well for them. My recommendation is to simply share your plan, but feel free to experiment with this step and find out what works for you.

The Power Morning

"The secret to your future is hidden in your daily routine." - Mike Murdock

Inspired by Hal Elrod

What do Barack Obama, Bill Gates, Oprah Winfrey, Mark Zuckerberg, Hal Elrod, Tony Robbins and other successful people all have in common? They all have a distinct morning routine they practice every single day. Barack Obama, as the President of the United States, was one of the busiest men in the world, but he still set aside two entire hours to himself each morning to get himself fully ready for the day ahead. When Hal Elrod was 20 years old, he was a successful salesman with a good life. In fact, he had just purchased his very own Ford Mustang. However, he had no idea that his comfortable life was about to get turned upside down—in fact, it would even stop for a moment. Driving at 70 mph, Hal was hit head on by a truck. He was clinically dead for over six minutes at the scene. When Hal came back to life, he entered into a six day coma. The doctors said it was a miracle for him to even be alive. In fact, they told him that he would never be able to walk or think correctly again. His brain was severely damaged. Despite the extreme adversity that Hal had to overcome, he is now a New York Times Bestselling author, motivational speaker, and has appeared on multiple TV shows.

Hal believes that the key to his success was the discovery of what he calls the Miracle Morning. The Miracle Morning is a morning routine that Hal created to help him defy the prognosis of the doctors and lead the life he so eagerly desired. I started practicing this morning routine as a twelve-year-old and it helped me far more than I could have ever imagined. Goals are fantastic, but this routine gave me a plan to execute, visualize, and empower my goals to make sure my mind was always on the task of achieving my greatest self. I have reaped staggering results by this daily habit. Everyday, I feel more centered and all of my actions are towards an ultimate goal. This morning routine changed my life, so I have taken inspiration from Hal's morning routine and created a morning routine that I am confident can change your life if properly applied. I call it the Power Morning.

The greatest thing about the Power Morning is that it starts your day out with all of your most important tasks. These tasks will never be taught to you in school and you have probably never practiced most of them before, but as you do, you will find how crucial they really are. The great thing is, with the Power Morning, you start your day out with an accomplishment. Before you even begin your day, you are successful. This starts you off on a positive and gets the momentum rolling. Another huge benefit of the Power Morning is that it will always keep you on track. You know how some days you are just not feeling it? This routine nearly entirely eliminates that feeling. This morning routine is based off of the acronym GOAL. By following these steps, you will not only see massive results—you will achieve your goals.

But before we get into the acronym, let's start with the night before your morning routine. It is extremely important to go to bed and wake up at around the same time each day. "Our sleep is closely tied to our circadian rhythm," says Dr. Robert Oexman, Director of the Sleep to Live Institute, over email. "When we change our sleep and wake time, we alter our circadian cycle. We experience this when we stay up later on the weekends and sleep in later in the morning. Most people find it difficult to fall asleep at bedtime on Sunday night and will often find it more difficult to wake up on Monday." A study published in BMC Public Health found that going to bed at different times is associated with poorer sleep quality and increased fatigue. "Altered sleep schedules, as seen with shift workers, is also associated with a greater risk of accidents, lower immune system, [higher] risk for chronic disease, and a shorter life expectancy," says Oexman. So: get a time that works with your schedule, and then stick to it. A great way to do this is to put an alarm on your phone not just to wake you up, but another as well to alert you of your bedtime.

These days, as teens, it is easy to get stuck in the habit of living on very little sleep at all. The National Sleep Foundation recommend 8-10 hours of sleep every night for teens. This recommendation was not just pulled out of a hat. If you are not getting this amount of sleep you will be much less effective in the time you actually are awake. Many people wear their lack of sleep as a badge of honor, doing so to show that they are grinding harder than everybody else. In reality, these people are risking their health and sacrificing their efficiency. Failure to get these 8-10 hours of sleep weakens your immune system, impairs brain function, creates moodiness and depression, weakens your memory, and is a leading cause of obesity. I know that with all of the homework and extracurricular activities high school demands, it can be extremely difficult to get the right amount of sleep, but if you want to be successful, it is important to recognize the importance of sleep.

The Power Morning

Okay, so let's get into the very first step of your power morning. Step one is to strategically watch how you go to bed the night before. First of all, never ever, no matter how tired you are, skip your nightly rituals. My nightly rituals include brushing my teeth, washing my face, and doing 25 pushups. This step may seem simple, but makes a world of a difference. Secondly, and this is really important, as you lay in bed, before falling asleep, be happy. Think about being excited to wake up the next day. You know how you feel on Christmas morning when you are exuberated and elated to be alive? Be like that: so excited for the day ahead of you. Think of the days you wake up depressed and how awful it feels to start out your day like that. Our goal is to wake you up every morning feeling excited to tackle your goals and make a difference in the world. If your goals and dreams don't make you want to leap out of bed in the morning, go find different ones. The trick to waking up with that feeling is to visualize your goals and get excited about them the night before. This is one of my favorite benefits of the Power Morning. I love the way it feels to wake up.

Step two is to wake up right. As soon as you wake up, smile no matter how you are feeling, ignore the snooze button, choose to be happy and hop right the heck out of bed. Then, make your bed. A staggering study by Hunch.com found that only 27 percent of people make their beds and that 71 percent of bedmakers consider themselves to be happy. On the other hand, 62 percent of people who don't make their bed admit to being unhappy. The fact that there is a direct correlation between happiness and making your bed should be reason enough. To add to that, this study found that bedmakers also have much more financially successful lives.

Finally, you are going to drink an entire cup of water to wake you up. While most of us are not very thirsty when we first wake up, we have been without drinking for (hopefully) eight hours and we are slightly dehydrated. By drinking water every morning, you will be rehydrating your body and waking yourself up fully. The next step in the Power Morning is where the acronym GOAL comes into play. As you practice your Power Morning, remember this acronym.

GOALS

Gratitude | Visualize and write down three things you are grateful for.

Optimization | Meditate and Exercise | Visualize your goals.

Affirmations | Repeat positive statements while looking in the mirror.

Learn | Read, educate and empower.

Scribe | Journal | Write down your goals.

Gratitude

G for gratitude. Once you've completed the steps mentioned in the previous section, find a quiet place to sit and reflect on what you are grateful for. Personally, I love sitting on my bed with crossed legs. If you do decide to sit on your bed, make certain that it is already meticulously made. Now think of three things you are grateful for—but don't just visualize it, become it. You have to step into the very thing you are grateful for. If you are grateful for a roller-coaster then imagine yourself in the seat, about to hit a dip in the ride. What does it feel like, smell like,

40

taste like, look like, or sound like? The clearer you can paint this picture the more effective the exercise will be. It is also extremely important to make one of these things simple. For example, this could be the sun, weather, or even the smile on your sibling's face.

Two of the biggest emotions that hold us back are fear and anger. I have often found that people tend to become reactive to these two emotions, which is a severe problem. If we are always reacting based off of our emotions, we will never be successful. Have you ever tried to be both grateful and angry at the same time? Have you ever been grateful and fearful at the same time? Undoubtedly, the answer is no. It is impossible to feel these emotions simultaneously.

Recently I had the opportunity to the race the 1600m at a stadium in Colorado. I have run this race a few times before, but this was different. I was facing off against the number one freshman in the US and was feeling horrible. My legs felt like Jello, I had gotten less than five hours of sleep the night before, and I was sure that I was about to barf. Needless to say, I thought it was hopeless. As we began our warmup, nothing changed. I just decided that I was going to do my best no matter how I felt. Although, I didn't think my best was going to good. Right before I walked onto the starting line, I was extraordinarily nervous. Then I remembered the advice given to me by sub 4 minute miler, Kyle Merber. After asking Kyle how he overcame the pre-race nerves and fear, he told me this: "There is nowhere else I'd rather be than on that starting line." We get so obsessed with our fear that we forget how it incredible it actually is to be in the present moment. As I stepped onto that starting line, I decided to change my fear into gratitude. I smiled, relaxed, and enjoyed the moment. When the gun went off, I ran the best race of my life and tied for the third fastest freshman mile time in the United States of America, with altitude conversion.

Tetris is a game where shapes fall from the ceiling and, as they fall, you can arrange and rotate them to fit together. The goal of the game is to fit as many pieces together as possible, but it may take a little thinking. A study was done on this game in which college students were brought into a room to play Tetris for a few hours. After playing Tetris for such a long period of time and then stopping, these students experienced something called a cognitive afterimage. When these students went to the store afterwards, their brains automatically began putting shapes together. They started to see the real world as a game of Tetris. Every time they came across a box, they couldn't help but noticing all of the little spots it would fit into. It was almost like OCD but a thousand times more intense.

Their brains were constantly scanning for patterns. What do we learn from the Tetris effect? When you begin to visualize and write down the three things you're grateful for every morning, you have to scan the world around you for the good. You are purposely attempting to find good in your life. As you do this every morning, your brain will begin to benefit from the Tetris effect, because it is constantly looking for a pattern. Rather than having to stop and think about all of the things you are grateful for, to see good, you will begin to notice that your brain is automatically, subconsciously scanning for good 24/7. Imagine how much happier life would be if you developed this habit. Train your brain to scan for the good, and optimism and happiness will find you. Optimistic and happy people in turn find both success and form rich friendships.

7 scientifically proven benefits of gratitude:

- Gratitude opens the door to more relationships
- Improves physical health
- Improves psychological health
- Enhances empathy

- And reduces aggression
- Improves sleep
- Improves self-esteem.

Optimize

O is for optimize. In optimize, there are three tasks that must be completed: Meditation, Exercise, and Visualization. All three steps are mainly focused on optimizing your brain power for the day ahead. Firstly, meditation. Now, when I say meditation, most of you are probably beginning to tune me out because of the stereotypes. But just because you meditate doesn't mean you automatically become a spiritual, vegetarian, essential oils lover. Hey, I know a ton of cool dudes who meditate. Maybe you've heard of them: Mahatma Ghandi, Russel Brand, Tom Hanks, Clint Eastwood, Tim Ferris, Tom Brady, Hugh Jackman. Stick with me here, and I can convince you how much happier mediation will make you if you chose to allow it.

Our era is so busy. The pace of life is extremely hectic. Our brains are constantly doing and thinking. When was the last time you took ten minutes to do absolutely nothing? Not reading, eating, texting, tweeting or even pondering your past or future? My bet is that it's been a very long time. The mind is our most valuable asset and possession. Everything we experience comes from our brain. Every thought, decision, and emotion starts with the human brain. I find it miraculous how little we do to take care of the most important thing in the universe.

"The result, of course, is that we get stressed. You know, the mind whizzes away like a washing machine going round and round, lots of difficult, confusing emotions, and we don't really know how to deal with that. And the sad fact is that we are so distracted that we're no longer present in the world in which we live. We miss out on the things that are most important to us, and the crazy thing is that everybody just assumes, that's the way life is, so we've just kind of got to get on with it. That's really not how it has to be." - Andy Puddicombe.

Our mind becomes overwhelmed by the sea of thoughts it has to sort through. Think about it: the average person has up to 60,000 thoughts, makes about 35,000 decisions, and sees about 5,000 ads per day. Doesn't that seem like it would fog your brain up a bit? This fog has terrible after-effects and can lead to depression.

I have four incredible older sisters. One day, my oldest sister, Paris, had a college friend come to visit us for dinner. I was about 11 years old at the time and really looked up this 20-year-old girl. At dinner, my mom asked her what her biggest regret was from the last few years of her life. I never forgot what she said. It stuck with me for the next five years of life. She said: "I spent so much time being excited for the future and worrying about the past that I forgot to enjoy the present moment." The present moment is severely underrated. How much time do we spend dwelling on the past and anticipating the future? While sometimes this is important, we would do well to love and enjoy the moments that we live in, right now. There was a research paper that came out of Harvard recently that said on average our minds are lost in thought almost 47 percent of the time. Yes, 47 percent. At the same time, this sort of constant mind-wandering is also a direct cause of unhappiness. To spend almost half of our life lost in thought seems tragic, actually, especially when there's something we can do about it—when there's a positive, practical, achievable, scientifically-proven technique which allows our mind to be more healthy, to be more mindful and less distracted. The solution is meditation.

When I first heard of meditation I saw it as a voodoo practice for crazy people, but as I researched it more, all of the facts told me that I ought to give it a try. I fell in love with meditation. It's one thing to hear the facts and another to experience them. As I started to develop a daily habit of meditation, I almost immediately noticed a change in how much more calm, relieved, and patient I was. After about a year of me meditating consistently, my family could easily tell the difference between the days I was and was not meditating. On the no-meditation days, I was more angry, impatient, and rude than usual. I could not wait to try it for my pre-race and pre-game routine. It worked. Meditation reduces stress, and aging as well as improving attention span, metabolism, happiness, immunity, and even helps increase willpower.

Put it Into Action

So, I've given you the reasons—it's time to make it happen. There are three different ways I like to meditate, but they all include being in the present moment. You are not supposed to be thinking, pondering, or even praying during your meditation. This is to give your mind a break. I always sit with my legs crossed on my made bed as I meditate. My favorite way to meditate is through an app called Headspace. Download it on the app store and you will love it. The second way I meditate is with a brain scanner called Muse. This is not absolutely necessary, but is very helpful. Finally, the last way I like to meditate is unguided. I like to just sit on my bed, breathe in for five seconds and then out for eight seconds, and repeat. And yes, I know, that's a big stinkin breath!

Step two of optimization is exercise. In just about all of my first 15 interviews, my guests made a point of saying that exercise was a key habit that led them to be successful. If you are not willing to take care of your health, the rest of your life will suffer. In addition to the obvious benefits of being healthy and exercising, early morning exercise gets your brain pumping and your day started right. It helps your brain focus on the tasks that lie ahead. I can see a very tangible difference in my day from when I exercise as opposed to when I don't. For me, I don't really need more exercise. My average day usually consists of about six miles of running, a full basketball practice and sometimes even weight lifting. So rather than doing a full-on workout when I wake up, I just do 25 solid push-ups and six pull-ups. This little habit has worked miracles for me.

The final step of optimization is visualization. Visualization is a powerful tool that so many people underutilize, or don't utilize at all. Michael Phelps is the most decorated Olympian in history. He has won 23 gold medals and has 28 Olympic medals in total. Michael Phelps is arguably the most dominant athlete in history. Obviously there are many reasons why Michael Phelps is where he is today, but visualization might just be the thing that gives him the edge. In short-distance swimming, a fraction of a second could mean the difference between a gold medal and not even getting on the podium. He is known for being one of the most mentally-prepared athletes there is. Every single day, he spends two whole hours mentally rehearsing and visualizing himself in the pool. He hears the crowd, smells the chlorine in the air, tastes the water, sees the clock, and feels the excitement of coming in first place. Bob Bowman, Michael Phelp's coach, says that mental rehearsal is a proven, well-established technique to achieve peak performance in nearly every endeavor: "The brain cannot distinguish between something that's vividly imagined and something that's real." In order to make your dream a reality, you have to vividly visualize it as one.

Lewis Howes is a New York Times Bestselling author, seven figure income entrepreneur, and an Olympic handball player. But this is not where he started. When Lewis was 20, he was living on his sister's couch with no business experience and a broken arm. Here is the crazy part: Lewis set a goal to write a New York Times Bestseller. He visualized this goal every single day. He visualized himself walking into Barnes and Noble and seeing his book at the front of the bookstore with the bestseller label. He put himself into the moment everyday as the first

49

thing he did. It fired him up. I am extraordinarily grateful that Lewis set this goal. He played an astronomical role in inspiring me to write this book. When Lewis's book first came out, he went on a book tour to speak and answer questions. My mom, some good friends, and I drove about an hour away to the Barnes and Noble where he was introducing his book. I can't even describe the feeling I got from listening to this guy who is absolutely on fire and living the life of his dreams. He reminded me of everything I wanted to be later in life. I visualize being in that exact spot every day and it makes me jump out of bed with excitement.

VISUALIZE YOUR GOALS EVERYDAY!

Affirmations

A is for affirmations. After trying to convince my family for almost a year to try affirmations, I finally got my mom to do it. We were in Florida at the time on a family vacation and at about seven in the morning my mom shoved open the doors and almost started singing: "I am brimming with energy and overflowing with joy." Needless to say, she was annoyingly obsessed with her new discovery. Affirmations change you and your perspective on the world. First off, what are affirmations? I'm glad you asked. Well, at least I hope you asked. Affirmations are the process of affirming something to yourself over and over again. Here's how you do it. First, you pick an area of your life that you need to improve.

For example, I used to have an extremely difficult time loving people. It was the weirdest thing, and I hated it. So I recognized my problem, and I created an affirmation that would help me to get over this. This affirmation was: "I love everyone I come in contact with; I am a people person." So when I got to the affirmations step of my Power Morning, I would stand up in front of the mirror, smile, and repeat this affirmation about four times to myself in different tones of voice. This attempt was a major success! (Otherwise I probably wouldn't be telling you about it.) I can honestly say now that I love people and I am constantly gaining new friends because of this quality. My love for people has lead me to a much happier and more accepting lifestyle. Today, I have about 15 different affirmations that I repeat to myself while standing awkwardly in front of the mirror. Trust me: it might be strange at first, but after a little while it's not so bad.

We talked earlier about how achieving a goal is impossible without making your goals a standard. You have to make your goals a part of you. You will always be consistent with the person you believe you are. Affirmations are meant to shape this view to perspective. This form of positive self-talk is meant to change how you see yourself and how you react to the world around you—and believe me, it works. I can honestly say that affirmations are even more important that goal setting for most people. The way you see yourself and the world needs to be positive. I believe that confidence is one of the most important human attributes and this method helps improve your self-image and confidence. Affirmations can literally rewire your neural pathways. Change the way you think!

10 Examples of Life Changing Affirmations

1. Creative energy surges through me and leads me to new and brilliant ideas.

2. My efforts are being supported by the universe, and my dreams manifest into reality before my eyes.

3. I am proactive and productive.

4. I have a brilliant mind.

5. I am confident.

6. Many people recognize my worth; I am admired.

7. Today, I am brimming with energy and over-flowing with joy.

8. I was born to achieve greatness.

9. I am a difference maker and a world changer.

10. I am a magnet for success.

Learn and Scribe

L is for Learn and S is for Scribe. Those are the final two steps to the Power Morning. To learn is to read or listen to something that makes you better. I usually use this section to read my scriptures and listen to a personal development podcast or talk while I clean my room. Knowledge and action is power. The scribe step is to journal, plan your day, and write down your goals. If you are less talented, smaller, less educated and less experienced, you will always win if you are the one writing down your goals 365 days a year. This step will reaffirm and solidify your goals in your mind. It will give you brain something to search for. It will ultimately put cause your subconscious mind to focus on your goals. I am not as great at journaling as I would like to admit. I do journal, but not on a daily basis. But I've found an app that works well for me as an alternative. This app is called 1 second everyday. It allows me to record a 1 second video of every day of my life. I can then put little notes under the day to give myself a little journal of what I did that day. I would highly recommend 1 second everyday if, like me, you're not the best journal-keeper in the world.

The last step of your Power Morning is to plan your day. I recommend getting a notebook that you use to plan your day everyday. This step is crucial for living an efficient, productive and fun day. First, you are going to write down all of the things you need to get done that day. For all of the things you must get done that day, put an A in front of it. For things that you would like to get done but don't necessarily have to be done that day, put a B in front of them. Lastly, write down a few Cs—these are things that you can't do that day. Based off this list you just made, you are going to plan out your day by the half hour. Your highest priorities go first in your day.

How To Plan Your Day (Ex-ample)

A: Go to Dentist

A: Workout

A: Personal Basketball Practice

A: The Power Morning

B: Read an inspirational book

B: Help Friend Move

B: Practice the Piano

B: Brainstorm business ideas

B: Develop meaningful relationship/friends

C: Watch Netflix

C: Play NBA 2k17

6-7: The Power Morning

7-8: Workout

8-8:30: Eat breakfast

8:30-9: Shower/ Get ready for the day

9:30-11: Dentist

11-12: Basketball Drills

12-12:30: Lunch while listening to podcast

12:30-1: Practice Piano

1-2: Brainstorm business ideas

2-4: Help Friend Move

4-6: Team Basketball Practice

6-10: Dinner and Hangout with Friends

Fully Written Out Power Morning (30ish minutes)

1. Go to bed strategically, be excited to wake up in the morning and never skip nightly rituals.

2. Jump out of bed, smile no matter what, and make your bed. Lastly, drink a cup of water.

3. G:ratitude: Write down and step into the moment of three things you are grateful for.

4. O:ptimize: Visualize your goals | Meditate for 5-10 min | Exercise.

5. A:ffirmations: Stand in front of the mirror and repeat your 10-20 affirmations.

6. L:earn: Read a book, listen to a podcast, or educate yourself in some way.

7. S:cribe: Write down your goals, journal, and plan your day.

    I can tell you from personal experience that, if you let it, the Power Morning can change your life. Make it a habit in your life. Every time you miss a day, it makes it harder to do the next, then harder to do the next, and then even harder to do the next—and soon enough you won't be doing it all. Do whatever you can to never miss a day and you will see the results in yourself. I always find it best to do your 30-45 minute Power Morning early. It feels much more powerful the earlier you do it. Doing it later in the day can make it feel ineffective and a waste of time. The biggest excuse of all time is that you don't have time. Find time to make this work and schedule a consistent time for you to practice your Power Morning. I can't wait to hear about how this changes your life!

Comfort Zone

"Whoever fails the most wins." - Seth Godin

Inspired by Jia Jiang

The comfort zone separates the greats from the average people: the average people hide in the comfort zone, while the greats flee from it, searching for something more challenging. I've seen it happen a thousand times in real time, right before my eyes, in basketball practice. What happens is the coach lines all the players up in a line and has them do a series of simple ball handling drills. Some players think the drill is easy, and they dribble the ball softly. The second group of players dribbles just hard enough to make it difficult. But the best players, the ones for whom it should be easy, dribble the ball as hard as they can while keeping their head up and their posture perfect. These players lose the ball more, mess up more, and embarrass themselves a lot more. They turn a seemingly simple drill into a difficult one. They push themselves to their absolute limit so they can get the most out of each drill. These are the players that have the most success throughout their basketball careers. Two things we can learn from this: success is in the details and pushing yourself (or, in other words, getting outside of the comfort zone) brings success. No matter how much talent that first group of boys have, they will never be as good as the boys who pounded the basketball.

The comfort zone holds so many of us back from achieving our greatest potential. When I first started my podcast, it scared the heck out of me. I didn't want to be the weird homeschooled, vegan, podcast kid. Especially being on a basketball team that would undoubtedly give me crap if they found out I had a podcast. Being different is scary. In fact, sometimes being different is absolutely terrifying.

Dare to be different. These four words have always been so inspirational for me. Have you ever met a difference maker, somebody who was changing the world, that did things just like everybody else? No, of course you haven't. They don't exist. If you want the same results as everybody else, then take the same route as everybody else. There is no way to exceed mediocrity by doing the same thing as everybody else. The key to success is to be extreme. Successful people go all in, they go extreme, and they make no apologies for it. Think about it: Steve Jobs dropped out of college, everyone told him he was a fool for doing it—and then he founded Apple.

Steve Prefontaine, one of the most famous runners to ever live, ran in a way that was considered flat out stupid: he would run his guts out from the start, rather than saving it all for the last minute. Craig Sager was one of the most famous reporters of all time, and he was unafraid to be himself. He wore funky clothes and lived his life the way he wanted to. If you want to have massive success, you have to be different. To have different results, you have to take different action.

I have been getting a ton of questions recently about my education, diet, business and book. So here it is: In the sixth grade I made a choice that everybody thought was absolutely ridiculous. It was risky, untested and unknown. I decided to do online school. At the time I was extremely passionate about entrepreneurship, as well as learning how I could live my life to the fullest. Those two years of online school were spent getting as far ahead as I could in school as well as avidly reading any self-help book I could find and looking for my first business opportunity. Online school brought me the freedom to follow my passions to the absolute fullest and also taught me that I didn't have to do what everybody else did. I realized that if I wanted to be great, I had to take great action and do things differently. The combination of this realization with the boost that online school gave me made me decide to skip high school altogether and become a full time college student at 14 years old. So I did. I also got a little outside of my comfort zone and discovered that I could mesh my love for entrepreneurship and personal development into one project. This is where the idea of starting a podcast came into play. Now, I get to interview people that have made it. I get to follow the roadmap of the greats.

But this was nowhere near easy for me. It was extremely scary at first to get outside of my comfort zone and personally ask guests to come on my podcast—and then even scarier still when the time came to interview them. As a 15-year-old highschooler, this was terrifyingly outside my comfort zone. This journey of podcasting has allowed me to learn so much —about myself, the guests and about life—that it has all been worth it. Right now, I have written my very first book, I'm preparing to (hopefully) give a TED talk, and I'm working on developing a goal-setting course for teens. Besides all that, I'm a nationally-ranked plant-based vegan runner. Ya, I'm weird and I absolutely love it. Find out what makes you weird, because without your weird, you are holding back your greatness. The weird people are the ones who change the world. The world is always pushing you to be normal. I am far from normal and unfortunately sometimes that means more than the fair share of crap, but it's all worth it.

Whenever you do something abnormal, when you push the status quo, it will upset some people. Here is what I have learned over the last few years. Everybody is trying to build their tower and climb up in the food chain. If they see your tower is higher than theirs, they will want to tear yours down. This fact has caused me to lose some great friends. While it's important to recognize how you may be making others feel, it's always important to recognize that the people who want to tear you down may not be as good friends as you think they are. When you do things that are brave, cool, different and successful, you will lose some friends and find others that are much more like you. You don't have to walk on the well-beaten path just because everyone around you is. Go off the path. Explore. Get lost. Find yourself again. Be different.

Conquering Fear

One quality about myself that I sometimes find difficult is that I am extremely sensitive. This quality can often be a challenge for me. Whenever I face rejection in my life, it hurts badly. A few years ago I told a friend that I looked up to about my goal to become a BYU basketball player one day. He gave it to me straight. His response was that I wasn't genetically capable of the goal. He said that I couldn't jump high enough, run fast enough, or shoot well enough to ever achieve this goal. This crushed me. I didn't even want to play basketball for a month after that. Your path to greatness is going to pass by people who will tell you it is impossible.

Kyle Maynard is a man in his 30s with no arms and no legs. He is a quadruple amputee with aspirations like you wouldn't believe. How many people do you think told him along the way that what he wanted to do was impossible? Today, Kyle is the only quadruple amputee to have climbed Mount Kilimanjaro without prosthetics and has also won an ESPY as a mixed martial arts athlete. This is when you put rejection aside, laugh and go get that dream. Overcoming your fear of failure—and unwillingness to fail—is one of the key components to living a successful life. The more you fail, the more likely you are to eventually succeed.

Have you ever been afraid of rejection? I certainly have. Whether it's talking to a girl, asking for a favor, making a sales call or going for a job interview, we all have something we are too afraid to do because of the fear of rejection. About a year ago, I came across a TED talk that completely changed my perspective on rejection. Jia Jiang is an Asian-American that was too afraid of rejection to find success in his life. He let fear dictate the person he became. This fear is the biggest reason we stay in our comfort zone. When Jia Jiang discovered he was being held back by his fear of rejection, he decided he needed to make a change. As a result, he decided that he was going to look for rejection. For 100 days straight, Jia would ask random people for strange things in the hope of dissipating his fear. On the first day he asked to borrow $100 from a security guard. As expected, the man said no. Jia apologized immediately and ran away. On another day, he went to a burger place and asked for a burger refill, but got the same response. But as the days passed, he started to gain confidence and actually started to get a lot of yesses. theOWhen he got a no, he would keep trying. Statistics have shown that the average salesman makes the sale on the seventh try. Jia persisted with his ridiculous requests and people finally started giving in. I absolutely loved this idea when I first heard it, so I tried it out for myself. It was ridiculous and funny, yes, but it really did help me get over my fear of rejection. My challenge to you guys is try Jia's "Rejection Therapy". Challenge yourself to get rejected for rejection's sake. It makes all the difference in the world—and it's fun!

Performance

"Whether you think you can or whether you think you can't, you're right". - Henry Ford

Inspired by Amy Cuddy

The Southwest Region Nike Cross Nationals was one of the most surreal experiences of my life. I had been preparing for this race since I was ten years old. The healthy eating, the long runs, the meditation, the visualization: it was all in preparation for this race. When I was younger, I loved to run, but it wasn't for cross country: it was for basketball. I would run as hard as I could for about two miles once or twice a week just to stay in shape for basketball. I can distinctly remember coming home from runs and feeling so proud of myself. I would sit at the kitchen table and rave to my family about my five minute miles on the trail—even though they didn't believe me. I tried out for middle school track about a year later, unsure of how I would do. To my amazement, I ran the course a minute and a half faster than my peers and then later went on to get second at the middle school state meet.

Fast forward to my freshman year. I continued to work hard and eat extremely healthily. My goal at the beginning of the cross country season was always to win the NXR race in November; however, I had no idea if it was possible. I had many people tell me that I had no chance and one friend even began naming all of the people he knew were going to crush me at this race. It was definitely a lofty goal, but I kept doing the small things—the one percent of things—that very few were willing to do: ice baths, vegan, sugar-free eating, visualization, and goal setting. In the end, it was all of those small things that made the biggest difference. As the date drew nearer, I was ready both physically and mentally. I flew into Phoenix two days before the event and visited the course the night before the big race. The course was exactly what I had visualized it to be. When we pulled up to the course, I had the most surreal, indescribable feeling. It felt so right. Rather than the usual nervous nausea and dizziness, I couldn't wait to make my lofty vision become a reality. I spent the rest of the night drinking nasty beet juice, eating wholegrain bread, and getting my mind prepared.

I woke up bright and early the next morning to drive to the course. The hours leading up to the race consisted of quite a bit of prayer, stretching, meditating, and plenty of bathroom breaks. Thirty seconds till the gun goes off. I was standing on that line squashed in between 500 kids, just waiting for that gun to off so I could make a full out sprint. The tension was unbearable, but I felt ready. The gun went off and all 500 boys started running, fighting for space. I had already made my way to the front by the 100-meter mark by weaving in and out of people. By mile one, I had established myself in the top five as we ran our first split at 4:54 —my personal best for a mile. I knew I was in for a race. Constant cheering from coaches on the sideline kept me going as the fatigue set in. At mile two, I wanted to quit. Me and two other competitors had pulled away from the mass of people. The quick start had drained me, but I was not giving up. I just kept repeating positive quotes to myself over and over: "Pain is temporary, pride is forever," and "A minute of pain is worth a lifetime of glory," both by Louis Zamperini. At mile three, with one tenth of a mile to go, I pulled away for good and ran guts out. I crossed the finish line first, winning by a margin of six seconds. I was elated. It was such an incredible feeling to have all that work pay off. I was swept up in a big hug by my parents. This was easily one of the most rewarding experiences of my entire life.

In life, we are constantly asked to perform. Whether it be piano, a test, an interview, an athletic event, or bakeoff, you will have to perform. Lady Gaga, Michael Phelps, Tom Brady, Lindsey Stirling,

Michael Jordan are all some of the best performers in the world at what they do. The question is, what makes them so great? These successful individuals have mastered the flow. They can get in the flow when a game winner is needed or when there is only a lap to go. Obviously there was more that went into their success than their ability to get into the flow, but this is a staggeringly large part of their success. When in the flow state, you are five times more effective.

I have had a lot of ups and downs playing basketball. In sixth and seventh grade I can remember working my butt off at becoming the best basketball player possible. I put way more hours in the gym than anybody else my age. I would wake up every morning at 5:30 to go to the gym for an hour to put shots up. I would spend an entire hour just doing shooting drills. Then, I would come back to the gym at four in the afternoon and do ball handling and finishing drills with a coach. Lastly, I would either stay at the gym and wait for the next drills session at 6:30, or go to the rec center and play one versus one to put my skills to the test. I was a good basketball player, but I wasn't great. I would work my butt off and then in games or tryouts for teams, I would blow it. I was the best player in the gym at drills, but could never play well when I needed to. I was hurt and discouraged. I would play ball with all these kids who sometimes shot around with their brothers after school, but never did drills, yet they were out-performing me in games.

I can distinctly remember one of the most discouraging moments of my life. I was in seventh grade and had joined a new basketball team. I was so excited to have made this team because it was arguably one of the top three basketball teams in the state of Colorado for our age group. After playing with this team for about two months, we made the trip to Portland, Oregon to play in a national tournament. I couldn't wait to have all my hard work pay off. I started the game on the bench, which wasn't too surprising, but after the first quarter I hadn't even been in the game. I was bummed, but thought I would for sure go in at the start of the second quarter. Nope, I went all four quarters without ever stepping on the court. I was devastated, absolutely crushed. The second game went similarly, except that my coach put me in for the last 30 seconds of the game so he could say he did. After working as hard as I had, I couldn't understand why this was happening to me. I was working with all the best coaches and doing everything they told me to do. I realize now that this excruciating trial was largely due to my inability to perform. I didn't know how to obtain the right mindset in order to play my best. After experimenting for years with both basketball and running strategies, I learned what works best in order to enter the flow state.

The Power Pose

In June 2012, a social psychologist, Amy Cuddy, gave a TED talk on the topic of body language. This TED changed the way I think about my body language. Our body language or nonverbal cues, as well as those of others, shape meaningful outcomes in our life. We subconsciously judge others based off of their nonverbals. This can lead to large life decisions like who we choose as friends, who we ask out, or who we promote. A study done by Nalini Ambadi, a researcher at Tufts University shows that when people watch a 30 second soundless clip of real physician-to-patient interactions, their judgments of the physician's friendliness was a good predictor of whether or not he would be sued. Even more dramatic is the example from Alex Todorov at Princeton. His studies have shown that the judgments of political candidates faces in just one second predict 70 percent of US senate and gubernatorial race outcomes.

When animals need to seem powerful, they make themselves look bigger, they open up, spread out, and take up more space. When the cobra is threatened and wants to intimidate its assailant, it flattens out its ribs, making it look much larger. Humans do the same when they feel powerful. Whenever we feel prideful, we naturally feel the need to spread ourselves out and make ourselves larger. This is why Usain Bolt spreads his famously long arms out after winning all his races. Blind people—people who have never seen this behavior—have the same reaction when they win. They put their arms in the air and lift their chin up high. Just as our own nonverbals have an effect on others, they can also have an effect on ourselves. What about when we feel defeated, sad, or weak? We make ourselves smaller. We shrink up. We don't wanna bump into the person next to us, we slouch over, or we hang our heads. Watch out for this and you will see it. Next time you walk into your classroom, by observing body language you will be able to immediately see who the alpha in the room is. You will also be able to see who is feeling nervous and who lacks confidence. The alphas will typically be taking up a lot of space and spreading themselves out, whereas the less confident people will make themselves seem smaller.

Cool stuff right? Here is why it matters: you can fake it till you make it. A good example: when you are sad, if you smile for 30 seconds, you can trick your mind into being happy. There are so many times that we feel sad and defeated. The last thing you want to do when you are in one of these moods is to smile. It feels absolutely horrific and wrong at first, but then you will begin to find that it is actually changing your mood and making you happier. When you force yourself to smile, your brain releases dopamine, making you happier. This simple tip has worked miracles in my life. Try it.

In the same way, you can boost your confidence by practicing what Amy Cuddy calls power poses. These poses are anything that makes you bigger and take up more space. Let's say you have been chosen to give a huge speech presenting your business at an out of state event. You are feeling nervous and anxious and scared. Here's what you do: on the car drive to the event, you spread your legs out and put your hands behind your head for about two minutes. A power pose like this will result in a boost of confidence and authority for you. A study showed that after practicing the power pose for only two minutes, testosterone levels rise and cortisol levels fall, reflecting a sensation of confidence and power. I have used this in my life—before races and basketball games and other stressful activities—and it makes a world of difference. I can't wait for you to try it in yours. Pretend to be powerful and you will feel powerful. Fake it till you make it. Fake it till you become it.

The Power of the Mind

The first step in leveraging your performance is to recognize your why. It takes motivation to be successful. Without a drive or a reason to become successful, you will never arrive at your desired destination. It takes so much work and so much sacrifice to achieve your goals that you can't possibly find the motivation without knowing what your why is. Wanting more money is not enough. The drive for money is not sustainable. If you want to live a life of complete success, you must find your purpose. I don't know what your why is and maybe you don't either, but I do know that when—not if—you face challenges, when you simply don't want to do what it takes, money will not be motivation enough. Your why can surely contain selfish motives, but it must include a bigger purpose as well. My older sister, Savanna, went on a service trip to an orphanage in Ecuador when she was in high school. During this month long trip, she grew close to many of these children. When she left, she found out the orphanage was running out of funds and would soon have to transfer all of these kids to a significantly less suitable home. Savanna is now in college, with very little money, yet she donates $1 for every sale she makes in her own successful company, Tossd Salt Spray, to this orphanage. She has built up this successful business for the past two years and has donated almost $5,000 to the orphanage—all while attending college. She found her purpose on a trip to Ecuador as a teenager, and that has been the key to her success.

Our minds are so terribly underrated. The definition of Placebo is a fake treatment. I want to talk to you about something called the Placebo effect. Countless studies have been produced in which doctors prescribe placebos to see if the patient reacted. When these patients are given the placebo and told that they are receiving a pill that will dampen their conditions, the patient's report to feeling better. In another example a man with cancer is told that he is being given a cure for his brain tumor. While this cure was fake, the results were astonishing. After less than a week, this man was acting completely normal and his brains tumor had literally shrunk. 3 days later he discovered that the cure was fake and immediately became sick again as the tumor expanded. There have also been incredible results with placebos and curing poison ivy.

The four-minute mile was a human barrier considered impossible to achieve. So many made an attempt, yet nobody could break it. Scientists had deemed the human body incapable of such a feat. The athletes believed them. Roger Bannister was the first man to dip under four minutes. He had achieved the impossible. But this where it gets interesting: as soon as Roger Bannister proved that it could be done, John Landy dipped under four-minute mark in the same year. Today, breaking four is the standard of professional distance runners and the record now stands 17 seconds faster than four minutes. What was holding us back from breaking the four-minute mark? Whatever it was, it obviously wasn't physical—it was all in the mind.

Usually when a professional athlete achieves something like this, or really any feat or victory, they are interviewed. In these interviews the athlete almost always gives one of two responses: they thank god for their achievement or they say they're the best of the best and nobody will ever beat me. This response is particularly prevalent in the world of boxing. Muhammed Ali was one of the best boxers of all time and was known for boasting that he was unbeatable. While this was may have come across as arrogant to many, it played a big role in his success as a fighter. The greatest athletes know they will win. If you can work hard and convince your mind to believe that you will win, your mind will find ways to make success possible. The power of belief is immeasurable.

Wim Hof, or the iceman, is a dutch man that holds 26 different world records related to extreme cold. He has buried himself wearing only a speedo in an ice tank for almost two hours. He has climbed Mt. Kilimanjaro with nothing but swim trunks and he has the world record for longest distance swam under ice. This man does things that are not physiologically possible. How does he do it? Wim claims that the key to his feats have been the mastering of his mind and breathing techniques. There is plenty of evidence that the mind is powerful, yet so few people use it to their advantage. The trick is to find a balance between reality and positivity. Keep reality in mind, sure, and always remember your limits—but then try to break through them.

The thing I love about running is that it is so relatable to life. There are so many lessons that we can learn from the beautiful sport. In the 8th grade, I ran in the Colorado Middle School State Championships. I wanted more than anything to place first at this meet. A few extended family members had flown out to see the race and I was determined to push myself as far as I could go to get this win. I ran just about the entire race in second place until the last 200 meters, when I made my move to pull ahead for the win. As I went to pass the front runner, the guy in first place made a surge for the finish line. He stayed half a stride ahead of me in a full out sprint for about 100 meters, and I broke down mentally. I was pushing my hardest and I just couldn't get ahead of him. I didn't realize this when I was running, but looking back on it now, I see where I failed.

Physically, it was 100 percent possible for me to continue my all out sprint for at least 100 more meters. That is why milers always go all out for only the last 200 meters. Runners have about 200 meters of anaerobic strength and I had only used about half of that reserve when I gave up. It wasn't that I couldn't do it—it was his half a stride on me that destroyed me mentally. I believe that if I had kept up with him for about five more seconds, he would've been the one to give. This doesn't just apply to running. Sometimes, in life, we give up five seconds before success. Our hardest moments were the most crucial moments, the ones when we just needed to push through to see success around the corner. Don't ever let adversity be anything but an opportunity for you. Don't let your mind let you down. Don't beat yourself. Find a way to win.

The Compound Effect

"The people who are crazy enough to think they can change the world, are the ones that do."-Steve Jobs

Inspired by Darren Hardy

There is no big secret to success. Success lives in the little things in life. So often our focus is on massive change. We tend to believe that we can only find success through inventing the atomic bomb, so to speak. It's easy to think that a single event is what makes people rich and famous. Without a doubt, many businessmen, actors, and athletes can become successful or famous off of a single event, but they didn't just arrive at the opportunity. What you don't see is what it took for them to get to that point. These people became successful as a result of the small and simple daily choices they have made and that have had created a domino effect in their lives. This book is all about helping you to step outside of the comfort zone, challenge the status quo, and live your dream life. I believe that the best way to get where you want to go is by appreciating the details and making the small and simple changes in your life that will ultimately change it. I want to share with you two things that have been inspired by Darren Hardy and The Slight Edge, by Jeff Olson.

The water hyacinth is an absolutely astonishing plant that floats on top of the water in warm areas of the world. This plant has a beautiful and unique flower with purple leaves. The water hyacinth is one of the fastest-growing plants in the world. A single water hyacinth can produce up to 5000 seeds, as well as sending out short stems that become new plants. The water hyacinth doubles itself over time. One plant becomes two, two become four, four become eight, and so on. On the first day, the water hyacinth is unnoticeable in a large pond. By day four, having doubled four times, it is still unnoticeable, and after 20 days it can barely be spotted from a distance. But by day 30, the water hyacinth will have completely covered the entire pond, making it impossible to ignore. Over the course of your life, you will find that you are not much different than this exotic plant. The decisions you make everyday will not be noticeable at all—until they are impossible to ignore. If you choose to make the extra little effort and make the small and simple choices to be better, you might not see any change day to day—but you will see results in ten years that are undeniable.

Let's say you are flying across the country from California to Ohio to play a lacrosse game. The plane you board is in perfect condition, except for one little mistake: the nose of the plane is one degree off. Nobody notices—it's only one degree. But by the time you are supposed to be landing, you will have ended up 150 miles south of your destination. That one degree was imperceptibly small at first, but over time it led you to being a full state away from your desired destination. How do the most successful people in the world arrive at where they are today? They don't perform heroic feats, they don't take quantum leaps, and they don't become successful overnight, but they do make the small and seemingly insignificant choices that lead them to success.

You go to a restaurant for lunch and you are presented with a menu. Do you go for the hamburger and fries or do you order the salad? Now, this doesn't seem like a decision that is going to alter your life forever or bring you massive success. At the end of the day, do you go to the gym and get a workout in and then knock out some push-ups before bed? Or do you rush home to catch up your favorite TV show? It's not a big deal, right? Yet it's the small and seemingly insignificant choices such as these that make the biggest difference. In the heat of an argument, do you allow yourself to get riled up and angry, or do you be the bigger man or woman and apologize for

81

your wrongdoings? At your athletic practice, do you go your hardest or do you give yourself just one more easy day? Small and seemingly insignificant choices lead to big results.

If I were to offer you a penny that doubled every day for 31 days or an immediate lump sum of three million dollars, which would you take? Well, let's think about it. Let's say you picked the penny and your friend picked the three million. Five days go by and you've now got 16 cents and your friend is partying it up like a rockstar with his millions. Ten days go by and you now have a whopping $5.12. Your friend is now on a yacht in the Bahamas and you can't afford a happy meal at McDonalds. A lot of people would give up at this point. By day 20, you now have $5,000, which is still nothing in comparison. But by day 31, your penny has turned into $10,737,418 compared to your friend's now-meager three million dollars. This is why Darren Hardy said compound choices are the eighth wonder of the world.

Finally, let's take three individuals who are prime examples of Darren Hardy's compound effect. These three individuals all live similar lifestyles. Each is a real estate investor with two children. One day, Scott starts listening to my Fueled podcast and decides he wants to make some minor adjustments in his life. So he decides he is going to start doing these few things: each day, he is going to read ten pages of a self-help book, park at the back of the parking lot and take the stairs, eat 125 fewer calories, and make just a few more sales calls. Scott is obviously not looking for a major life transformation in his life—he's just making some extremely achievable adjustments. Anybody can do this. Larry is going to maintain the status quo and not make any changes. Lastly, we have Brad. Brad decides to make the opposite adjustments to Scott: he is going to munch on a little bit of junk food at work, drink a little more diet coke, skip a few workout days, and skip a prospecting call or two everyday. No big deal right?

Five months after these adjustments, these three friends look exactly the same. Ten whole months down the road and still no difference whatsoever is apparent in their appearance, income or health. Scott is extremely discouraged at this point, but continues his new adjustments. Now 20 months after the adjustments, the results are just slight: Scott has lost a little weight and Brad has gained a little. It's not until 27 months until Scott starts seeing dramatic results and Brad really starts to regret the decisions he has been making. By now, Scott has read over 47 books—the average college graduate reads less than three books for the rest of their life— on personal development, lost 63.5 lbs, and increased his income by almost $300,000. I'm sure you can imagine the opposite effects on Brad. Let's not go into the ugly details.

It's the small and seemingly insignificant choices that will change your life. The crazy thing about these small differences are that they are easy to do and easy not to do. By becoming aware of these things and becoming more conscious of your choices, you can create transformation in your life. Always recognize that the choices you make today will have an effect on your future, no matter how small. Lastly, when you make these small adjustments in your life, they become habits and create a positive momentum that will lead to more and more positive change.

The hardest thing about making these small choices is that the results seem to be invisible. I am currently 5'10", but I certainly wasn't born that way. The impact these choices have in your life are so gradual, that they are unnoticeable in the moment and can only been seen if you are looking back. Unfortunately, most of us have developed a strong desire for immediate gratification over all else. If I were to offer you $100 right now or $200 in a year, most would take the $100. We take the smaller reward with quicker results. If all you learned from this book was to be patient and take actions that benefit your future self rather than your present self, you would walk away a happier and much more successful person. To do this, it takes discipline.

Discipline is involved in every action you take as a human being. All of the best athletes, musicians, actors, and businessmen have mastered the art of discipline. It requires discipline to get out of bed every morning, eat healthy, workout, practice, and to do the things that ultimately separate you as a great. Muhammad Ali said it best: "I hated every early morning workout that I have done, but I love being a world champion." One of the greatest boxers of all time, Muhammad Ali, recognized that he needed to have the discipline to do what nobody else wanted to do so that he could have the results that nobody else got. He did things that were excruciating in the present moment so that he could live a historical future.

I want to give you three steps to developing discipline. Step one is to be motivated. I believe a big part of why so many people struggle to get where they want to go and to complete the necessary tasks is that they lack motivation. Hard work without motivation and purpose is impossible. The best way I have found to stay motivated is to get excited and visualize your goals achieved. Whenever I am having a tough time putting in the work at a track practice, I visualize myself crossing the finish line and gliding through the tape as the crowd cheers and the clock reads that I have run a sub-four-minute mile. Step two to developing discipline is to find the activity that gets you out of your slump. Do you ever have days where you just can't think straight and have no desire to do your homework or to practice the piano or to do whatever you have to do? I certainly do. I have found that the best solution to this is to find an activity that gives you momentum and gets your brain pumping again. For me, this can be to mow the lawn, go on a long run, or shovel the driveway. The key to productivity is momentum. Once you complete a small task, your big tasks become more achievable.

The final step to developing greater discipline is to put yourself first and time-block your day. What is the first thing you do every morning? Most of us have developed the habit of grabbing our phones and checking Instagram as our very first action of the day. This is an absolutely horrific start to your day. I would recommend that as soon as you wake up, you need to get right into your productive day while leaving your phone unchecked for at least the first thirty minutes. I have spent so many hours in my room doing school work and working on my podcast. Since I do not go to school, it can often be difficult to manage my day and stay productive. Highschoolers wake up at about the same time every single day and go to school at about the same time everyday. My schooling is a little different: I often don't have due dates, and I do not have a set time that school starts. For a very long time, this hurt me. I was unable to get much done and I had an extremely difficult time being productive.

After a lot experimenting, I have learned all of the most effective ways to manage your time and to be productive. First off, schedule your day into time blocks. There are certain things that need to be done everyday. For me, this is school or working on my business. Everyday, I have a mandatory appointment with myself starting at 8:30 in the morning. If you set a consistent time for your activities, you are significantly more likely to get them done. Remember in the chapter about the Power Morning how I taught you how to plan your day by getting the most difficult things done first? If you schedule out your day, you will find that your productivity will skyrocket. Procrastination kills.

Fun fact about me: if I am not productive and progressing, I become extremely stressed and unhappy. Without progress, happiness becomes extremely difficult to achieve. This is why binge-watching Netflix or hitting up 2k17 is such a bad idea. Believe me, I have done both, but I always find myself in a worse mood afterwards. Obviously taking breaks and watching a movie every once in a while is not a bad thing, but it is best used as a reward after a productive, hard-working day. If you want to be happy, cut out the things like Netflix and 2k that are disguised as things that will make you happy. If you want to be happy, work your butt off towards something that you are passionate about. Seek to make a difference in the world. Progress is happiness, so find ways to progress every single day.

Success is not easy. There really is no shortcut to success. Despite what some will tell us or what we would like to believe, success is painful. It takes blood, sweat, and tears. Even going beyond that, life is painful. It all just depends on which pain you prefer. Which suffering suits you the best? Do you prefer the pain of waking up at 5 in the morning and grinding all day long for your goals, or do you prefer the pain of being overweight, poor, and mediocre? To be great, you have to be willing to suffer and sacrifice. Every workout hurts, but so does being 100lbs overweight. Studying, reading and learning can be painful, but it brings great reward. "Suffer now, and live the rest of your life a champion," as Muhammad Ali said. Success is not easy, but it's worth it.

The biggest excuse of all time is that you don't have time. I don't have time to workout after school, I don't have time to make healthy foods, I don't have time to put that extra hour in after practice, I don't have time to meditate, I don't have time to read. If you don't have time to do these things, you will never achieve greatness. Plain and simple: all of these little things that take a little extra time are what will sepa-rate you. These little things will shoot you to the top like you wouldn't believe, but apparently there is just not enough time. There is always a way to make time. If you want to achieve greatness, you are going to have figure out how to make time. Think about all of the time you spend entertaining yourself everyday. Tomorrow, carry a stopwatch around with you. Stop the timer for every second that you are not being productive. You will be amazed by how little time you spend being productive. There is always a way to find more time for your priorities.

Excuses are a plague of success. You are re-sponsible for everything that you are. You are the reason you look the way you look. You are the reason you didn't make that team. You are the reason you are not winning. It doesn't matter where you come from, who you live with, or what your circumstances are. We live in a generation in which there is an ex-cuse for everything. You will never be successful if you continue to blame your failure on others. If you want to be great, it is nobody's job but yours to make sure it happens. Excuses sound best to those who make them. When you choose to see everything as negative, as an excuse, nothing will move in your life. You will stay the way you are and never improve. To change your mind is to change your life. Get rid of the negative outlet and start seeing solutions rather than excuses. Have you ever purchased a course or program that claimed it would change your life in thirty days? How did that go for you? There are hundreds of thousands of courses out there and billions taking them. The most common response to these supposedly life-changing courses are that they are faulty. People are almost always unsatisfied with their results and blame it all on the program. Here is the thing: programs cannot have any chance of functioning without a high quality operating system. We all have the resources and the knowledge to do whatever we want in our lives, but it's up to us to make it happen.

How to Develop Meaningful Relationships and Gain Influence

"You are the average of the 5 people you spend the most time with" - Jim Rohn

Inspired by Dale Carnegie

The older I get, the more I realize the true value of people. Think about it: everything you have came from someone else. The world revolves around people. I believe that the ability to win friends and influence people is the most important skill in the entire world. If you have good people skills, you can make anything happen. I'll be totally honest with you, this chapter is not as entertaining as some of the others, but it might just be the most important if properly applied. My brother in law, Pierce, is a prime example of this. Pierce is one of the most socially adept people I have ever met. He is constantly introducing himself to new people and is always interested in the lives of those around him. Pierce is a smart guy, but everything he has is a direct result of his ability to gain friends. He built a business around featuring cool companies by making friends with the owners. He and my sister have a wedding photography business that creates all sales through people that they have met and become friends with. Somehow, Pierce is always getting hooked up with great deals for random stuff and saving tons of money in the process. Finally, he has a fantastic circle of friends who are all doing cool things with their lives. If you can learn to develop fantastic people skills, you can do anything you want in life. I can't even tell you how many times I have been provided an opportunity that never would have arrived without my understanding of people.

Jim Rohn said, "You are the average of the five people you spend the most time with." All successful people surround themselves with the difference makers. If you want to change the world, start hanging around those who already have. If you are hanging around five billionaires, chances are you going to be the sixth. If you are hanging around five pessimistic, negative, sad people, chances are you going to be the sixth. The way you talk, walk and act are almost always a direct result of the people you spend the most time with.

Genie Wiley is a feral child with an absolutely horrific story. Genie lived the first 14 years of her life locked up in her dark bedroom with almost zero human communication. When the police discovered that Genie was being abused, they immediately brought her in for medical attention. After being alive for almost 14 years, Genie could not perform any basic skills like speak, walk, or even properly use the restroom. Genie had nobody to learn from. Humans are experts at mirroring others. Our brains cannot properly function without the examples of those around us. Genie's tragic story is proof that we will become like the people around us. Sometimes, as a highschooler, it can be difficult to find people with the big aspirations and dreams that you have. While friends do not need to be perfect, it's important to recognize if they are positive or negative, optimistic or pessimistic, happy or sad, driven or lazy. Choose your friends carefully and you will never regret it.

Smiling is severely underrated. We talked earlier about how faking a smile can actually trick you into being happy. Going beyond that, a smile is a magical way to get people to like you. When you smile at someone, it shows that you are happy to meet them. People like to be appreciated and when you smile at them, it makes them feel appreciated. As you begin to make a habit of smiling more, you will notice that it feels a little awkward at first, but you will find that people smile back. Its incredible how such a small action can create such a large result. Babies are the perfect example of this concept. No matter what mood you are in, when you see a baby smile at you, you can't help but smile back and be happy.

Professor James V. McConnell, a psychologist at the University of Michigan, expressed his feelings about a smile. "People who smile," he said, "tend to manage, teach, and sell more effectively and to raise happier children." There is far more information in a smile than a frown. This is why encouragement is much more effective than punishment. Everybody wants to feel loved, and a smile makes them feel just that. Many telephone companies have their phone representatives smile while talking on the phone with their customers because their smile comes through their voice and makes their customer feel appreciated and important. I would even recommend trying this with family members and friends when answering the phone. When you answer, do so with a smile on your face and excitement in your voice. Put a reminder on your phone to smile and you will be amazed at the results.

Develop an Interest in Others

To understand how to win friends and influence people, it is important to study the greatest winner of friends the world has ever known. I want to share with you a brilliant story written by Dale Carnegie as it a perfect display of influence. "You may see him tomorrow and when you get close to him, he will begin to wag his tail and run towards you. If you stop to pat him, he will always jump out of his skin to show how much he loves you. Behind this dog's affection are no ulterior motives. He doesn't want to sell you anything or marry you. Dogs are the only animals in the world that do not have to work for a living. A pig makes for some good ribs, cows make milk, and chicken lays eggs, but the dog has no such responsibility. Dogs make their living through nothing except love." - Dale Carnegie | Everybody loves dogs, but why? We love people who are interested in us. This is an important lesson to understand.

You can make more friends in two months by becoming interested in others than you can make in two years by trying to make others interested interested in you. People are not interested in us—they are interested in themselves. The most common word used over telephones in the US is the pronoun I. When you see a group photo that you are in, whose picture do you look for first? If you are always trying to make others interested in you, you will never make any real friends. It is the person with the least interest in other people's lives that has the greatest difficulty in life. We all like to talk about ourselves. The best way to make a friend and create a good first impression is to talk about them while developing an interest in them and their life. Have you ever been at dinner with a friend and all they did the entire time was talk about themselves? It's enough to make you never want to talk to that person again. By asking questions and becoming involved in others lives, you make them feel loved and important.

Make Others Feel Important

Think of the most liked or popular person that you know. What do all of these people have in common? Each and every one of these people are experts at making the people around them feel important. At parties, these people go out of their way to compliment you and make you feel loved. My oldest sister, Paris, is an expert at this. Every time she greets someone, she does so with a compliment and a smile. The thing is, she means it too. Flattery is never an efficient strategy. You have to find something that you sincerely love about the person you are with and be confident enough to let them know you appreciate whatever it is. People are experts at seeing through flattery and it ends up doing more harm than good. A simple, sincere compliment can make somebody's day and create a new friend. I put this theory to test last summer when I went door to door around the neighborhood offering to power wash trash cans. I found that when I made my sales pitch after first giving the person who answered the door a sincere genuine compliment, my sales doubled. Think about all of the good you can do in the world by simply giving someone a little attention and appreciation. Sometimes a compliment takes confidence, but remember: people like people who like them.

How to Get What YOU Want

Our lives can often feel like a series of sales pitches. If you are a teenager and don't think you are in the business of sales, you are wrong. Whether you are trying to convince your parents to let you go out on Friday night, or getting that boy or girl to notice you, sales will be inevitable. We are always trying to get things from other people. If you are not good at convincing people of what you want, you will never be living the life that you want to live. The trick to sales is to recognize what the other person wants as opposed to asking for what you want. Arouse in the person an eager want. If you can do this, the world will open up to you. In Dale Carnegie's book How to Win Friends and Influence People, he talks about a young boy that was unhealthy and underweight. His parents would scold him about all of the things they wanted him to eat without any regard to what the boy wanted. This tends to be the most common approach. Not surprisingly, the boy wasn't convinced.

After weeks of riding his son about his food, he started to think about how the boy would benefit if he ate a little healthier. Rather than thinking about what he wanted, he started to think about what the boy wanted. His boy had a tricycle that he loved to ride up and down the street on, but a few doors down lived a bully, who would pull the boy off of the tricycle and put himself on. The boy was devastated and angry every time this occurred. Recognizing this, the father explained that the boy would be able to beat the crap out of the bully one day soon if he would only eat his vegetables. The following day, the boy ate all of his vegetables and begged for more because he would do anything to beat that bully.

This is true for all of us. The trick to getting what you want is not to convince others of what you want, but find what they want and tell them how you can help them get it. Merge your desires into what you both want. A deal that is better off for you will almost never be made. People are interested in what they want and people like to be a part of the solution. The best way to convince someone to do what you want is to have them come up with the solution.

Make them feel like it was their idea. How many times have your parents been mad at you or told you to do something that you didn't understand? My parents are incredible, but this happens to me too and I absolutely hate it. The more effective way to do it is to state the problem and have them help you with the solution.

Nobody ever thinks that they are wrong. Arguments would never occur if one person always admitted to being wrong. The worst criminals in the world believe that they have done nothing wrong. Terrorists, more often than not, convince themselves that they are doing the right thing. This is why criticism is an extremely negative tool. Think about one of the many times you have been criticized. Rather than making you change your mind or attitude, it makes you angry and defensive. I have four sisters and this can be a challenge for me. I often find fault in my sisters and find it extremely difficult not to criticize them, but criticism does nothing but hurt relationships. So if you cannot criticize, what can you do? There are three things: let them be part of the solution, sell them on what they want, and recognize their perspective. All of us could do a better job at understanding the positions of the people around us. Understanding the opposing point of view will allow you to understand that every action has a reason behind it and sometimes people need love rather than criticism.

Nobody knows the true cause of insanity, but we do know that over half of the world's insane people have nothing organically wrong with their brains. Mental illness is more common in the US than all other diseases combined. Many doctors believe that the true cause of insanity is the need for attention. Doctors believe that in the depths of insanity, these people crave appreciation, love and attention. The number one reason for divorce in the US is lack of attention from the spouse. One of my sisters used to have a code word for when she needed more attention. Humans live off attention. This is one more reason to say hi and smile at the people you pass by. The more friends that you acquire, the more opportunities you will find and the happier you will be. I'm not saying that you need to have one million friends that you hangout with every weekend and know every detail of their life. If you just take the time to remembers someone's name and a few other small things about them, it will be of much advantage to you both.

People are fantastic and there is something to learn from everyone. The more friends you have, the bigger impact you will be able to make. Many marketers, entrepreneurs and salesman make "friend making" a massive part of their job. People bring success. The point is not to manipulate people into becoming just a pawn in your success—the point is to make a difference and actually become interested in, serve, and learn to love the people around you.

Be genuine about it and connect with people. People love to hear their own names. Names are precious. Next time you meet someone new, make a special effort to memorize their name and pronounce it perfectly. Then, make an effort to say their name often when addressing them, as opposed to a nickname or something like dude, man, or bro. It will make them feel important and that is the ultimate goal. The unfortunate side to names is that when you forget them, you can hurt people. Here is the trick: when you meet a new person, memorize their name and then write it down as soon as their back is turned. If it is a hard name to pronounce, ask them to spell it for you. Teddy Roosevelt, the 26th president of the United States, was an expert with people. He new every cook, maid, florist, and janitor's name in the Whitehouse. Can you imagine how special you would feel if the President of the United States knew your name? He would address each of these people everyday when he saw them. Next time you pass someone that you know—or even just kind of know—in a hallway, make an effort to stop and say hello with a smile on your face.

Introduce yourself to as many people as possible. It takes confidence and often requires you to get outside of your comfort zone, but there is absolutely zero negative effect of getting to know another friendly face. You never know who might just end up being a lifelong friend. If not, maybe you will make someone's day by making them feel important. If you want to be successful, you have to become an expert in dealing with people. If you can learn to make others feel important, you will have the entire world opened up to you. Be real, be friendly, and make real friends.

OBSESSION

"No one is going to hand me success. I must go out and get it myself. That's why I'm here. To dominate. To conquer. Both the world and myself." - Lewis Howes

Inspired by Caleb Maddix

Personal development is incredible. There are so many things you can do to make your life better, like meditation, visualization, the Power Morning, and other life-changing hacks. But no matter how many of these hacks you use, your success will ultimately boil down to belief and work ethic. Those who are obsessed with their goals are those who achieve them. If you work your butt off with the mindset and belief that you can do and be anything, then you undoubtedly will. Every successful person is obsessed with their goals. Steve Jobs once went three days without sleeping while working on the iPhone. Beyonce didn't eat for two days when working on a new album. All of the greats we know, every name that ever will and ever has gone down in history, are great thanks to the fact that they were obsessive.

Caleb Maddix is a 15-year-old entrepreneur that is currently closing on making his first million dollars. I mentioned earlier that I interview him for my podcast back when I was just getting started. I learnt three important lessons from that interview:

Lesson one: The way you treat people is important. The second I met Caleb, he was on a constant mission to make me feel good about myself. He was one of the kindest people I have ever met and it has undoubtedly played a huge role in his success. If you listen to our interview, the first minute is simply him complimenting me and telling me about all the things I was doing well. This made me love the guy. It's so much easier to appreciate someone when they appreciate you.

Lesson two: Successful people are obsessive about their goals. They will work their butts off to achieve what they desire. The theme of Caleb's entire interview was built on obsession. A few years ago, Caleb developed an obsession for magic, did nearly nothing else for a year, and he became incredible at it. Another year he chose to master baseball because he thought he wanted to play in the MLB. He would wake up every morning at five and hone his craft. He would always pick one single thing and pour his heart into it. This is the way life should be lived. No matter what you are doing, no matter what your dream is, become obsessed with it. Take the actions that nobody else will and get the results that nobody else can. How bad do you want to succeed? Whoever wants it and fights for it the most will find it.

Lesson three: If you want something, go and get it today. Or as Caleb put it: "The gun that kills the most people is the gunna." When you say that you are gonna do something, it'll never happen. If you want to write a book, if you want to start making some serious money, if you want to start a business, stop saying that you are gonna do it. Do it. It doesn't matter how old you are. There is no such thing as being too old or too young to start working towards the things you desire. Gonna almost always becomes never.

A few months ago I had an incredible opportunity. After quite a bit of work, I was able to get Jimmer Fredette on my podcast, Fueled For Teens. Jimmer is one of the guys that's made it. In college, he absolutely demolished the rest of the NCAA basketball league, won the league's MVP and then went on to be drafted to the NBA. Now, Jimmer plays basketball in China—and he's the defending MVP of the league. This interview was particularly exciting for me because I really looked up to this guy. Before interviewing him, I had seen him multiple times and observed that he was one of the nicest people I'd ever seen. You'd think that a guy as accomplished as him would be stuck up and proud, but he was the just opposite. There were so many qualities in him that I wished to acquire myself.

During my interview with Jimmer, I asked him what made him special as a basketball player. Basketball is one of the most competitive sports in the world, with tens of millions of people trying to make it to the top. Out of these people, only about 300 people make it. This means only about 0.002 percent of people who have the dream to go big in basketball actually make it. Obviously Jimmer had figured something out. I assumed he was going to tell me about some insane training secret or some magic shot making product, but I was completely wrong. Jimmer's life changing secret was that he worked harder than anybody. That's it: hard work. He put in more hours and worked day in and day out to make sure there was no way he would land anywhere but exactly where he wanted to go. The crazy part is, Jimmer is no athletic freak either. He isn't seven feet tall and he wasn't born dunking. When you want something bad enough, when you become obsessed with something, when you work harder than anybody else—that is when you will find success. You don't need a secret potion to be successful, but I guarantee that if you are willing to do the dirty work and work harder than anybody else around you, the results will come.

Willpower

Willpower is required in every action that we take. It takes willpower to get up in the morning, eat healthily, workout, and do the tasks that make our lives go round. It takes willpower to be great. In the 1960s, a Stanford professor conducted an experiment to test the willpower of four year old children. These children were placed in a room and sat down at a desk with a large marshmallow in front of them. These kids were told that if they waited for 15 minutes or so without eating the marshmallow, they would be rewarded with another. Many of these children ate the marshmallow as soon as the instructor left the room. Some just stared and watched the marshmallow. Some even began picking off pieces. Only about 30 percent of these four year olds had the willpower to wait out the 15 minutes. Many years later, the kids who were able to resist eating the marshmallow were significantly more successful in the real world. These kids had higher SAT scores, stayed fit, and obtained better jobs than those who could not resist the marshmallow.

Your success is a direct result of your willpower. It is a direct result of your ability to decline immediate gratification for an ultimately greater reward—for that second marshmallow. The American Psychological Association claims that willpower is actually a limited resource. Willpower is like a muscle. The more you use it, the more tired it gets. But it can also get stronger if you work at it. Every morning, you wake up with a certain amount and as you go throughout the day your willpower will drain. Every difficult choice we make sucks up a little bit of our literal, limited willpower supply. If you are offered a burger and fries in the morning but you say no, it will be more difficult to refuse if you get the same offer for lunch. Saying no takes willpower. If you say no to a billion things in the morning, it will make it impossible to say no to these things at night. Success has more to with what you don't do, than what you do do. When you understand that you don't have an unlimited supply of willpower, you can start to make a difference. The first thing you can do is remove the temptation. Remove the choice. I love chips. I eat so healthily, but chips are my weakness. Whenever we have them in the house, I eat them. So we don't keep them in the house anymore. If you want to become healthier, throw away the soda. It is extremely difficult to eat healthily when you open the fridge and see soda, frozen pizza, lunchables, chocolate milk and ice cream. Don't even give yourself the option to cheat. Remove the temptation and you will find that it makes worlds of a difference.

The second way to develop greater willpower is to get the hardest and most important things done first. We have talked about this quite a bit already, so I'll just breeze over it. Since you will most likely have a fairly small amount of willpower at night, get everything that is difficult and important done first. It will make the rest of the day so much easier. Procrastination is something that we all struggle with. I certainly do. We are constantly telling ourselves that we will do it tomorrow, but tomorrow always becomes the next day. The most successful people in the world have learned to get the hard things done in the here and now as opposed to never getting it done at all.

A third way to improve your willpower is to construct strong and positive habits. If we only have a certain, limited amount of willpower, are we all bound to only do a certain amount of good things in a day? Do we have to sacrifice some good choices for the benefit of our willpower? No, of course not. The key to all of this is habits. Habits are subconscious, which allows us to do them without having to make a choice. Some of us have bad habits like—as simple and small as it is—going to sleep without washing our face, brushing our teeth, or knocking out a few pushups. When we wake up, we have a habit of choosing to be lazy and laying in bed for just ten more minutes. Imagine how much better your life would be if you simply had the habit of jumping out of bed, smiling, knocking out 20 push-ups and reading a self-help book for a few minutes. We choose happiness. Every morning, as I wake up, I smile no matter how I feel and say to myself, "I choose happiness." Your life will be largely affected by your habits. Every month, choose only one or maybe two habits that you would like to acquire. This automation of good habits will help you to eliminate the use of willpower in doing things that make you better and move you towards your goals.

Your experiences in your life will be shaped by your approach. The way you approach things is everything. If you choose to view any activity as a negative one, it will be as such. The best example I can think of is that of Mondays. Everybody hates Monday, right? It's the the first day of the week where you have to get up on time and get your life back together after the weekend. People often hear somebody else talk about how awful Mondays are and then start to think about everything that's bad about Mondays for themselves. But before that it was just any old day of the week, same as the rest. Now, for the rest of their lives, they dread this day of the week. I'll tell you what: I love Mondays. Monday is the day that I get to kick start my week and put some work in. Monday is the day I start making a name for myself. If you approach anything in your life with a negative outlook, you will almost always receive a negative result. Positivity will create happiness in your life. Besides, your peers would much rather be around a positive you than a negative you. You don't have to be perfect, but there's no excuse for not being positive even when you're not.

Perfection is a myth. Sometimes it is extremely difficult for me to be vulnerable. I want people to see me as this perfect kid who is doing it all, but I make mistakes. I am nowhere near the realm of perfection. It has been a challenge for me to get rid of this image and open up to both myself and the people around me. When we expect to be perfect, we constantly let ourselves down. Often the world makes us feel like we need to look a certain way, act a certain way, or be a certain way to be great. We get stuck in a perfectionist prison that forces us to always put on a face that is not ours. As Lewis Howes said, "Greatness is not about being perfect, it's about being yourself, being imperfect, and being okay with those imperfections." Vulnerability becomes freedom. When you allow yourself to be vulnerable, you become more relatable and lovable. Everybody has flaws, sometimes more than just a few, but don't let these flaws hold you hostage. Never doubt yourself or be self-deprecating, but at the same time remember that it's okay to share your weaknesses.

The final thing I would like to share with you is the acronym CIA. CIA stands for Consistent Imperfect Action. Success is built on action. No matter how much you learn, you will never reach success without action. When I was first starting my podcast, I was caught in a quicksand of inaction. Every time I was unsure of something I was doing, I would stop. I was extremely inconsistent with my productivity and the work I was doing to get my podcast off the ground. I was trying to be perfect, and it was holding me back. I'd forgotten about Consistent Imperfect Action. Consistency is an attribute that all difference-makers have acquired. On the road to success, it's easy to want to be a perfectionist and make sure every action you take is the right one, but it's better to make a wrong decision than to make no decision at all. If I were going for a perfect book, this book would never be written. Do your best and move forward. You will make mistakes, but your forward movement will make up the difference.

If you have made it this far, if you have endured throughout this entire book, you are special because most won't even make it that far—and if you can't motivate yourself to finish a single book, how much further can you go? The things that I have taught you in this book are not mere theories of mine —they have been tested and proven countless times throughout not only my history, but the history of those who have made it to the top. My biggest hope is that you take the things you have learned from this book and take action. You are capable of greatness. Start following your dreams today. Start changing your mindsets, habits, and routines today. Start right now. I love and believe in you.

Made in the USA
Middletown, DE
22 February 2018